To my ~
special friend
Expect Miracles!
Mike
Doyle

MW01098957

DIVINE
INTERVENTION

A HAPPY RESULT OF PRE-PRAYING

MIKE DAIGLE

BALBOA.
PRESS
A DIVISION OF HAY HOUSE

Balboa Press books may be ordered through booksellers or by contacting:

Balboa Press
A Division of Hay House
1663 Liberty Drive
Bloomington, IN 47403
www.balboapress.com
1 (877) 407-4847

Because of the dynamic nature of the Internet, any web addresses or links contained in this book may have changed since publication and may no longer be valid. The views expressed in this work are solely those of the author and do not necessarily reflect the views of the publisher, and the publisher hereby disclaims any responsibility for them.

The author of this book does not dispense medical advice or prescribe the use of any technique as a form of treatment for physical, emotional, or medical problems without the advice of a physician, either directly or indirectly. The intent of the author is only to offer information of a general nature to help you in your quest for emotional and spiritual well-being. In the event you use any of the information in this book for yourself, which is your constitutional right, the author and the publisher assume no responsibility for your actions.

Any people depicted in stock imagery provided by Thinkstock are models, and such images are being used for illustrative purposes only.
Certain stock imagery © Thinkstock.

Print information available on the last page.

ISBN: 978-1-5043-9138-2 (sc)
ISBN: 978-1-5043-9140-5 (hc)
ISBN: 978-1-5043-9139-9 (e)

Library of Congress Control Number: 2017917369

Balboa Press rev. date: 12/14/2017

Contents

Opening Thoughts

If you are reading this, then you are in the right place. What follows is a collection of my real life experiences of having almost died, but in each instance, for some mysterious reason, I have survived. My hope is that what I share will enable others to overcome their own life challenge "obstacles" and live to see another day, so they may fulfill their own life purpose. There is much to learn in this classroom called life. It seems the more one understands the more minutiae there is to understand.

To start with, I began this life back in 1954. I am fortunate enough to have been born a fraternal twin. There's nothing quite like it in the whole world. In my opinion, it's the closest two people can be without being one person. I was what you would call a premature baby, weighing in at 3 pounds 2 ounces. I had to be housed in an incubator for many months following, just so I could survive, so I'm told. Funny how you remember specific things and how certain conversations have such a great effect on your life. I can still recall, just like it was yesterday, the doctor telling the nurse, who was fussing over me, "He's probably going to die anyway." I heard that and looked right in his face and decided right then "I'll show you! I'm going to live". You see, back in those days we didn't know much about smoking and how much it can affect a birth. My mom was a heavy 2 pack a day smoker back then and the Doc read her the riot act as soon as my twin sister and I were born. I'm told we came out black. Mom has told me the doctor told her that I would probably be blind and deaf by the age of four. That very day we were born she quit smoking, cold turkey. She never did smoke again. I still remember the carton of Salem cigarettes on top of the refrigerator at our home in Sacramento, California several years later. She had gone to the store prior to my birth and had purchased a fresh carton. I think they were about $3.50 a carton back then. She brought them home but hadn't yet opened them up. Years later this carton was still around, sitting on top of our refrigerator. One pack had been pulled out about an inch but it never was opened. Turns out this not only saved her life but those of all of us around her. I really admire my Mom for being so persistent by quitting like that and never going back. It taught me a VERY valuable lesson and as a result I am one of the most persistent people you will ever meet. This has come in handy many times and as you will see in the following pages Miracles have occurred as a result.

Life for me has been quite an event. You see, I've always felt like the "black sheep" in the family. Growing up, I went from being an ultra introvert, as I call it, to being quite the extrovert, at times. There was a time, even up through my teens, and even until I turned 20, that I had trouble even speaking with people. The world for me was filled with people playing tricks on me, people not being themselves, and I noticed that others always tried to be like someone else they liked. Yet, there were also those that were truly being who they were. I became quite curious why people acted the way they did and you could always find me in the family, not saying anything, but studying every single nuance of each and every one around me, even at the dinner table. It was plainly evident to me that I looked at life in a much different way than others, even in my own family. My birth dad died when I was 1 and my mom had the challenge of raising 6 children on her own, which included my twin sister and me. She did an excellent job of it. It wasn't easy. I remember eating quite a bit of peanut butter and jelly but we were always well cared for, and our relatives and our Grandma were always there to help out, whenever needed. We ended up moving from Hill Air Force Base in Ogden, Utah to Los Gatos, California. As time went by my mom got work and during the day my siblings and I stayed with the neighbors. Everyone helped out in any way they could and this was much appreciated by me and all my siblings. I don't know how we would have survived otherwise. Back in those days it was a different world. Moms stayed at home and raised the family. If for some reason the

Mom had to work, the other wives within a close distance helped out and carefully watched over the children and made sure everything was ok.

After 7 years of being a widower and being single, my Mom remarried. Pop was also a widower and was raising 2 children on his own. They met on a blind date. Things went well and before we knew it they were engaged. Imagine our surprise when a year later it was announced they were going to be married. And then, 1 year after that, my last brother was born. We now had a yours, mine, and ours family. What a menagerie it was! You had every single viewpoint you can imagine. Conservative, Liberal, you name it. It wasn't easy, but we all managed. I really don't know how my parents did it. I learned a great deal about patience from both of them and throughout my upbringing.

I bet you wonder why I say I grew up "different". Well, here is an example. I remember a time when I was 8 years old. The year was 1962. I was in the back yard of our home in Sacramento, California, where we had moved, after having lived in Los Gatos. I was having a nice visit with Mom. There was just the two of us. It was in the very early morning, and as we visited I mentioned how beautiful it was behind her. She asked me what I was talking about. "You know. The plants have dew on them and all have a glow of light around them." Mom looked at me again with that questioning look she gave me from time to time. I replied yet again, "You know. It's kind of like at church, and the circle of light around Mary and Jesus, but it isn't circular. As a matter of fact, you have it around you right now." Mom, being very protective of me, made me promise to never talk about what I was seeing with others. I asked why not. "Because others don't see what you see. They will think something is wrong with you and there might be trouble." Many years went by before I decided it was ok to communicate with others about this. I'm not saying I see things like this all the time. I don't. It comes and goes, but with practice and concentration it comes back easily. You may ask what changed my mind to make it ok to talk about these things. Well, I went to a live Channeling seminar, with Esther and Jerry Hicks. Esther channeled the beings Abraham. This was the first time they came to Portland and I wouldn't have missed this for the world.

As the saying goes, I've made it a point to always "take the road less traveled, and that has made all the difference". I guess you could say I am a spiritual explorer. I like to investigate mysteries and things of a nature that have never been solved, but I also make it a point to be well grounded with the "real" world also. Imagine yourself in my place. You grow up being "different" from everyone, and then it comes time to fly out of the nest and start to find your place in life. That was a real challenge for me. I was still very, very shy and I didn't know much about the material universe. I was however, willing and able to take on a new adventure. The year was 1974. One day, when I was 20, and still living at home in Sacramento, California, I picked up the local newspaper and started to look for apartments to rent. I found a nice one, not too far away, in the downtown area, for a very reasonable price, $120.00 per month. I announced to my parents right then and there I was moving out that very day. They both looked at each other in bewilderment and replied in unison "Oh?" I went to the apartment and the manager showed me around. Only one problem, it was TOO big! "Don't you have anything smaller?" "Actually, we do have another one that might be more to your liking." It was all fully furnished, with a Murphy bed, that came out of the wall, and it even had oil lamp lighting. I loved it. "This one is being rented for $100.00. What do you think?" I paid the man the money on the spot and started the big move. Finally, I was all settled in. Not a bad price for rent, don't you think?

Remember though, I was extremely shy. I couldn't be that way any more but what could I do? I had an idea that worked for me. I decided, right then, that I would get up and walk outside and just start talking with the first person I saw. So I did just that. I was miserably shaking uncontrollably at first and was very uncomfortable, but I pressed through this. Pretty soon, with practice, I was able to talk about all sorts of things with people and I no longer was afraid about what would happen or what anyone thought. It was just another mountain to climb...

You ask what I did for money. Well, I got a job as a file clerk, making $3.49 an hour, quite a good rate in those days. As life went by, I made sure I got my taste of a variety of jobs. I remember one time I found I had a fear of heights. What would I do about this? Well, here's what I did. I became an installer at a local architectural sheet metal roofing company. I remember the first time I got up on an iron beam. I was literally shaking at the knees. My roofing coworkers on the ground under me were asking me, "What's the matter?" I replied, "I'll be fine. Just give me a moment." Pretty soon I was walking confidently across the beam, just like the famous Karl Wallenda. I chuckled to myself and was very proud to have gotten over my fear. I was successful in the job and stayed doing that kind of work for 5 years. You can still see the buildings today that I helped build, spanning 7 states…

As the years went by I found myself in a variety of jobs: as a groundskeeper, taking care of 40 acres of farm land, as well as being the caretaker of a private formal garden. I was also a "cedar sider" and learned to work in a team of 2. For a short period I worked as a security guard at the local airport, screening personal luggage for hazardous material or weapons. I was a cashier, a proof reader, even a tennis instructor. I knew I had a weakness with communication so I got a job as a carpet cleaner at Sears Carpet and Upholstery Cleaning and found myself in this job for 23 years. I loved every minute of it. I was taught carpet cleaning, carpet stretching and repair, water damage, odor control and furniture cleaning. You name it. I was even given the chore of being the company "problem solver". Whenever there was a "challenge" customer, I was sent to sort things out and make sure the customer was completely satisfied and would be calling again the next time they needed their carpet or upholstery cleaned. I got to talk very intimately with others and found out there are many others like myself, who have had amazing life miracles or circumstances that they had to overcome to survive. But I was lucky. They were all willing to share with me what happened. I must be a good listener...

I've also had a difficult journey, as many others have, in the relationship department. I was married for many years, and we were very close at one point, but we grew apart. With time, we both have healed and remain as friends to this day. Life goes on, as it should.

I've always been filled with curiosity about why things happen the way they do and this book is part of that journey. One thing I know I did along the way, was to decide, early on, with great intention, and emotion, to always be protected, to surround myself with those from the light, whose guidance I trust implicitly. What I mean by this is to be guided by special spiritual teachers from the other side. I said quietly to myself, but with great intention, "I want to interact with the highest of the high, the holiest of the holy, the wisest of the wise." This, I would say, has come to fruition, as I am here at this moment, writing this to you. If I had not done this things would have turned out much differently and I would not have been able to communicate my experience to you in this manner...

Parents

Recently my Mom passed at the spry old age of 97. I couldn't have asked for a better Mom. She was patient, kind, loving and shared her wisdom openly, to anyone who was willing to hear it. I was given space to grow how and when I could. It must have been hard on Mom. She originally had the thinking that you only lived once and that was it. As time went by she came to the realization that there was way more to this thing called life. Each of her children has special gifts, of one type or another. A couple have dreams that do come true, from time to time. Some are real good with math. Others are good with people. Still others are good at dealing with life challenges. We all learned from each other. As each grew up and moved away the dynamic of the family home changed and adjusted. Must have been especially hard on my youngest brother, as by the time he was a teenager Mom and Pop were getting up there in age and it must have been tough getting questions answered about life and about work etc. I did my best to fill in the gaps when I came to visit but everyone I think took from the home experience something different. Mom was a GREAT cook. She could get by with almost any food materials and fix something that was simply out of this world: Pear pies, Depression era chocolate pies, and meals from all over the world. You never knew quite what was going to be next. My parents had a rule that it didn't matter if you didn't like the taste of something, you at least had to eat one bite of it. I used to hate Brussels sprouts. Now it's one of my favorites to eat. Go figure… Mom did the best she could to stabilize the family unit and she did such a good job. She set a very good example for all of us to follow.

So, back to the other part of the story, my mom's passing. It was a very touching and profound event. I drove in my car from my place in Oregon for 12 hours to be with her during her last days at her home in Sacramento. She had lived there from 1961 through 2015, a span of 54 years. Yes, she still lived in the very same home. What family could make it there, did so. The transition came over time and not like what I had expected or, for that matter, even imagined.

Mom loved the sound of wind chimes and the outdoors, so in the last week of her passing, a few times while I was there, my twin sister would lift her out of the bed and into a wheel chair and off we all went for a "random scoot" from the living room to the back of the house, down the two steps and out onto the concrete patio and then out into the back yard on to the soft cool green grass. Sometimes her caretakers would also do this. There, on the corner of the house, is a large wooden trellis with rose vines draped over and around it. On one corner is a full sounding metal wind chime, with a wooden center "gong", attached to a string, hanging from the inner center of the chime. My sister would help Mom lift her hand up to the wooden clacker and together they would ring that chime. My other sister and I were there and the four of us simply beamed when we heard that chime. What a pleasant sound that was… The reason I'm telling you this is as follows… The day before my Mom passed, some of my family were in the living room. My Mom lay there, in the center of the same room, in a bed, being now unable to speak out loud. Two of my sisters were sitting talking to each other, off to the side, in the corner of the living room. I was standing behind them nearby, observing them. To my left was a "pole" lamp, with 3 lights, and on the knob to switch the lights on hung a very small wind chime. I was maybe two feet away from it. All of a sudden the chime sounded with a "ding!" sound. My sisters both stopped talking and asked me why I rang the chime. "You see me over here, away from it. I didn't ring it." Mom! Somehow, with this small miracle, she had managed to get across to all of us she was still around and was ok. We all laughed….

This was such a special time. Many never get to experience what we did. You see, when I arrived to say goodbye to Mom, she was experiencing several realities. I could tell she was observing both the present physical reality, but at the same time something quite magical was also going on. One of the caretakers came up to me when my sisters weren't around and asked me directly, "Mike, do you know anything about a canoe?" "What do you mean?" I replied. "Well, your Mom yesterday was having this conversation with some guy and they were talking about a canoe. I asked both your sisters but neither one knew what she was talking about." "Oh, that's easy", I said. "She's talking with my dad. He died when

I was one. Mom at one point told me a bit about the circumstances surrounding their first night as a couple, on their honeymoon. Her dad, Austin Calderwood, packed a picnic lunch for the newlyweds, tablecloth, silverware and everything and put it all in one of those large wooden picnic baskets. Dad got a canoe and he helped Mom get in it and then he got in himself and he paddled them from the mainland in Maine to a place called Raspberry Island, off the coast. There is a cottage right near the water. It was there they spent their honeymoon. She's talking with him about that." You should have seen the look on the caretaker's face. Priceless.

It would have been precious enough with just this, but more was to happen… Mom was still alive and was laying there in the bed, in the center of the living room, with her eyes closed. My sister was sitting in a chair on the far side of her bed, up near her upper body, looking down upon her face. The caretaker was on the other side, in the same position, sitting in another chair and he too was looking in Mom's face. I was standing on the near side, about the level of Mom's knees. The caretaker felt uneasy, as I could tell he felt I should be sitting where he was, and he should be standing. I felt compelled for some reason to talk about this with him. "I know you think I should be sitting where you are and you should be standing, but it's ok. For some reason I need to be standing right here right now." Right then, the three of us noticed on Mom's forehead movement on the left side. It was like she wanted to scratch an itch. Her hands were straight and by the side of her body and a blanket covered all of her up, from her feet to her neck. We 3 all noticed her left hand ever so slowly push up from her side and slowly move forward towards her head, all the while still being covered by the blanket. It slid further and further, until it got to approximately chest level. As any normal people would do, my sister and the caretaker went to move the blanket back, so Mom could then easily reach the place to scratch. "What?" They pulled the blanket back and when they did so, the protrusion of the hand pushing up on the blanket simply disappeared and the blanket went flat. Mom's hands were STILL flat by the side of her body! (No, I'm not making this up.) So this third hand had been moving upward to help her scratch her forehead! All three of us sat/stood there with our jaws wide open. We had just witnessed a miracle. We all looked back at Mom's head. Just then, we all noticed what appeared to be the impression the size and shape of a thumb pushing gently in on the place where she wanted to scratch on her head. We all shook our heads and smiled… I excitedly exclaimed, "Did you see that? Wow, THAT was awesome!"

But there's more…. Most people know there's been a terrific drought in California for the past several years, but guess what happened. Two hours before my mom's passing the heaven's opened up and a tremendous downpour ensued. It hadn't rained at all in over a month but it continued until well after two hours of her passing. An absolute miracle… but something else happened. I went to sleep that night, shortly after mom's passing, and was just lying there in bed with my eyes open, thinking about all that had happened, when all of a sudden I heard this loud noise "Kaboom!" and this giant ball of white light entered the room from outside the house and through the slatted window coverings. I sat straight up in bed. MOM! I wondered if either of my sister's had seen anything like this so I asked them about it in the morning. "Did anything happen to either of you in the room you were in when you went to sleep last night?" I had slept in the corner of the first floor. Turns out my sister sleeping on the second floor, directly above me, saw and heard exactly what I did, in exactly the same way! I can't explain it. I only know it happened. Amazing....

I look back and I remember something else of pure delight and magic. I wanted to have a "one on one" talk with my Mom, but there was always someone around. I had just read in a book that if you get a chance, get everyone out of the room and say what you need to say to your loved one, by yourself. Well, I did just that. I shooed everyone out into another room at one point, so Mom and I could visit together, without any interruptions. I looked down on her sweet face and smiled. "Mom, I have a request. If you have the chance and you're able to, I want you to come visit me, when you get to the other side." "Oh? If I can, I will. How so?" she replied. "Well, I'd like you to appear as a hummingbird. That way I will know it's you." She smiled, laughed a moment, and replied "If it's possible and I can, I'll see if I can, but you didn't ask me how I would like to contact you." "Fair enough Mom. Tell me," I replied. "Well, if it is possible, I would like to tap you 3 times on your right shoulder and that way you'll not only know I'm still around but that I'm ok too." I looked at her, started shedding a tear or two, nodded my head yes, and said, "You got a deal Mom. I'll be expecting it." The night of her passing, in a few moments after she crossed over, a hummingbird flew into the camellia bush out front, landed on a branch, and peered in at the 3 of us there. What an awesome blessing!

Two weeks after her passing I was back home in my own place in Oregon. I was sound asleep and I was happily awakened in the early morning by, you guessed it, THREE TAPS ON MY RIGHT SHOULDER. I leaned to the right and opened my eyes, only no one was physically there.... I laughed and laughed. "Mom, you did it! Thank you."

So, you are wondering if I've had anything happen along these lines with either my step dad (Pop) or my birth father (Dad). You bet.

Dad died when I was 1, in a T33 jet accident, when part of the tail section flew off the plane in flight, and he had 4 seconds to survive. He, as co-pilot, and his pilot, also a Lieutenant Colonel in the United States Air Force, both perished in the crash. It took over 50 years for me to get to the truth of his death but with persistence and help from two sisters we got to the bottom of everything. My birth dad had an amazing life himself, but that is for another book...

We have a running joke in the family, because my

dad was a Navigator in WW2, that whenever we need a parking space, we simply say out loud or to ourselves, "Ok Dad, I need a parking space, right up front!" Suddenly, someone pulls out, believe it or not, right up front. We pull in to where they have just left and we always laugh with delight. I have also had other interactions with him in various ways.

One time I went to the Oregon Coast Aquarium with my twin sister. We hadn't visited in person with each other in some time but what was going to happen was something to remember… We headed out and made it to the coast in great time and had such fun visiting and catching up with each other. We had spent the day walking through the entire complex and we decided to end the day by looking at some tidal pools. We got our fill and it was starting to get late in the day. We both sat down for a moment to reflect on all we'd seen. We were happily laughing when this older gentleman came walking up to us. He had an Oregon Coast Aquarium name tag on, balding, plump and was very friendly, with a very jovial laugh. He asked if he could join us. "Sure," we replied. We spent the next 40 minutes talking about life, relationships, kids, you name it. He was very interested in all aspects of our lives and we spoke about all sorts of things. I could see my twin was starting to think something was odd, but she could see I was totally comfortable talking with him, so she joined in all the more. It was now time for the aquarium to close so we said our goodbyes and I shook his hand vigorously and we shared a big smile. He walked away and we headed for the turnstile. I was beaming with delight but my twin exclaimed, "That was odd!" She became quite curious so she stopped to ask the person in the front office about the man. She described his physical characteristics and the way he made us feel so much at home. "I think you should give that man a bonus. I came all the way from California and he spent a good 40 minutes talking to the two of us about all sorts of things." The lady at the desk didn't know the person my twin was speaking about. "Where did you say you saw him? We don't have anyone working for us that fits that description." Up she popped and she made us show her where we had talked. Upon arrival there, we noticed this young aquarium worker was now sitting. She asked him about the man. "I don't know anyone like that. I've been in this section all day." We felt confused and now very puzzled. What was THAT all about? But I secretly knew. We returned home to Portland and stopped in to visit a dear friend of mine. I rang the doorbell and she opened the door. The first words out of her mouth: "Did you meet anyone interesting today?" We were both speechless, looked at each other in bewilderment and didn't say one word. We waited intently for the next words that came out of her mouth. With a big smile she mentioned, "The man you were speaking with today for so long was your father." I rest my case…

Now with Pop, my step father, who raised me from the time I was 8, I got to be there near the time he passed. We both used to wake up very early in the morning before anyone else had woken up, and had morning coffee together. We talked about all sorts of things, but we both knew and it was plainly evident the end would soon be here. So we shared some intimate conversation and said our goodbyes. Later, I remember going to the hospital. There was Pop, with my sister sitting in one chair and my Mom in the other. I walked up to Pop and he opened his eyes and smiled. "Mike!" We visited for a moment or two. Then, his attention was taken. He suddenly looked past me and exclaimed "Elaine, I'll be with you soon!" Elaine was the name of his first wife. She had passed away many years before, in 1957, from a bolt of lightning. Pop had told me all about what had happened in one of our earlier discussions. I looked to where he was gazing, past me, but he was seeing a woman who I could not see. It was very evident this was the real deal. Again, I was being placed directly in the space of greatest learning. I looked at Pop, smiled, and said my goodbye. People always asked me why, out of all the family, I didn't go to the funeral. Well, Pop told me himself he didn't want a big deal to be made. The main thing is that we got to talk very closely when he was alive and we said all that needed to be said. I can't say enough good things about the job he did. It wasn't easy. It was a blended family, two from his first marriage, six of us from my Mom's first marriage, and then Mom and Pop had a child, to tie everything together. We always joked that we had a regular baseball team! This was very fitting, as we have always been fanatic San Francisco Giants baseball fans. It never made sense to me, while growing up, why when I was little and just learning to play baseball, that I wanted to play little league for the Sacramento Bees, while Pop insisted I play for the Seals. What I found out later in life is that his father's brother was none other than Charlie Graham, who was one of the 3 owners of the San Francisco Seals, of the Pacific Coast League in baseball. "Uncle Charlie", as he was called, played for the Boston Americans in 1906, who eventually became the Boston Red Sox. Pop would have all sorts of baseball stories, especially about Joe Dimaggio. You see, Joe was "discovered" by his Uncle Charlie Graham and played for him on the San Francisco Seals. Joe was such a good baseball player the New York Yankees took notice. Pretty soon there was talk he would be sold to the Yanks. He eventually was sold, for the price of fifty thousand dollars, quite a sum in those days… After that, he would come over to my Pop's childhood home in Sacramento from time to time and visit with the family. Boys would show up at the door, wanting Joe to show them some baseball tips outside. One day, he agreed to show them, but they didn't have a ball.

Joe, when he made it to the Yankees, had all of them sign a baseball and it was protectively enclosed, and sat on the mantelpiece at Pop's childhood home. Joe rushed in and before anyone could stop him, out came the ball and out the door it went, with Joe Dimaggio flipping it up and down in his hand. The kids shrieked with delight. That baseball was worth a lot of money and when Joe came back inside the whole family was not too pleased. The baseball was completely ruined. Joe, I'm told, didn't feel too good about what he had done and so later on got a new baseball and signed it himself and placed it back in it's place on the mantel.

So I ended up playing baseball for the little league Seals in Sacramento myself. I still remember that Seals emblem on the breast pocket. Pop was pleased as punch.

Pop did a great job as a stepdad. I remember times he lost his patience but with that menagerie no wonder. As he got older he mellowed completely and we got to a good place in our relationship.

So, I guess you could say I've been totally blessed, with miracles sprouting up all over the place. It's been a regular garden of delight.

I am most appreciative of all the gifts I have been given, but **especially** the gift of life.

The Miracle of Birth –
The Will to Survive

My mom was a two pack of cigarettes a day gal during the 9 months she was pregnant with my twin and I. No biggy. That's the past. I forgave her long ago. There was a great deal going on in her life at the time and I fully understand her reasons for doing what she did. Now, for those that think smoking won't harm a baby the following may be a revelation.

It was time to appear in the world. My twin came out first and 6 minutes later I also arrived. I weighed in at a whopping 3 pounds, 2 ounces. Back then, most babies this small didn't make it. We must have created quite a stir. You see, I don't think they expected twins…I was tucked in, hiding behind my twin when the birth monitor was shown, I'm told, so no one even had a clue there were two babies. Mom told me at one point that my twin and I held hands by my using my left hand and she, her right, as babies. That may be one reason I turned out left-handed.

Both my birth parents were of European origin. I've been told both my twin and I came out black in color, due to the cigarette smoke. Nurses running everywhere… There was one in particular that literally saved my life. You see, the male doctor had given up. Some things you never forget. I distinctly remember the voice of the man. "He's going to die anyway," as the charge nurse was making a fuss over me. The doctor turned his full attention towards my twin. I heard his comment and looked directly into his eyes and decided right then and there that I was going to survive, no matter what the circumstances. My angelic nurse, on the other hand, totally ignored his comment and made sure I had all the care I needed and downright REFUSED to give up on me. I've been told I was in an incubator for about 3 months. My dad came to visit me there in the hospital, while my Mom was kept busy at home with my twin. Imagine trying to bond with your mother after that amount of time. It took until later in life for this to happen, but it finally did. As for my dad, he died when I was a year and 3 months old. But we did get to spend that special time together and I fully bonded with him, so much so, that the bond never did break, even after death. Life was certainly a challenge...

My siblings tell me the doctor took my mom into a private room and scolded her for smoking during the pregnancy. "Do you realize your son, IF he lives, will probably be both blind and deaf by the age of 4? What were you thinking?" From that moment on mom never smoked again. That was over 60 years ago and she lived to be 97 years old! There was always a carton, unopened, of Salem cigarettes on top of our refrigerator, as a reminder to her, and bless her heart, she never opened up a pack, not even once. Yes, one pack was pulled out a bit, but you could see it was never ever opened. Back in those times a carton cost roughly $3.00. Quite a contrast to what it costs nowadays…

I will say I've had my share of challenges: Had to have Laser Eye Surgery on my eyes back in 2003, as I was pretty much legally blind; I have had hearing aids, as my hearing became progressively worse; I was sick all the time growing up - German measles, mumps, chicken pox, you name it; I had to overcome extreme shyness, the kind where you can't even talk to people; I used to have "hammer toes", where the foot digits grow to overlap each other; I had severe buck teeth and not only did I get braces to correct this, but I also had to go to a tongue thrusting therapist, Doctor Zickyfoose, to correct my swallowing incorrectly; I was cross eyed; I had "wandering eye" challenges, where one eye faces forward, looking at an object, and the other eye "wanders" all over the place; I even had the beginnings of Scoliosis and had to deal with that. There's more, but you get my drift. My saving grace has been my persistence and my outlook on life that "the glass is always half full, no matter what the circumstances". It isn't what happens to and with you that is important, but how you view those circumstances.

You'll keep being given the same life lessons until you "pass the grade" and move on to another "class". It's much better to "pre-pray" your life than just let things happen as they may. What I mean by this is to focus with great emotion and intention on what it is that you want to attract into your life, instead of falling into the trap of putting attention on what you don't want and focusing on that. I still have many life lessons to learn, just like anyone else, but I'm on my way to an even better life...

I made it a point to have a nice long talk with Mom later in life about all of this and we both made our peace. I let her know I forgave her and she smiled and thanked me. We then gave each other a big hug and healing has now taken place!

I want to mention, in passing, that sometimes one may wait too long before they say what they need to say. By then, many times it's too late. Take the time to make time for those that mean the world to you. Things can and often do change in an instant. There may not be the one chance to say what needs to be said. And if it so happens that you miss that chance, there is still a way to reconcile things. You simply write down what you need to say on a blank sheet of paper. Fold it up when you're done. Place it in an incense container, a fireplace or something similar and simply light a match to it, while saying a prayer. This makes a big difference...

High Flyer

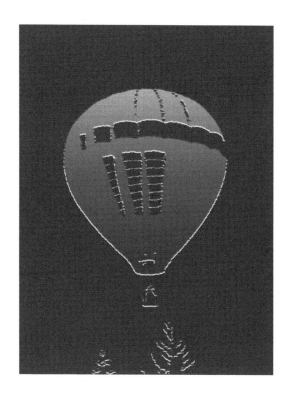

The year was 1962. I remember it was mid June. I was living at the time in Sacramento, California. It was a bright, scorching hot day, maybe 107. I was 8 years old at the time. Boy was I having fun. I had gone to the store and for 25 cents had gotten myself a High Flyer balsa wood glider plane! I came back home, ripped open the plastic wrap and put all the pieces together. I came outside and decided to enjoy the nice warm summer day and practice some tricks. I went to the nearest corner and got ready for my fun adventure. With my left hand I pointed up to the sky. With my right I held the glider and threw it up into the sky and it did a few loop-de-loops and gently floated back down to earth. I then tried an inside barrel roll a few times. Pretty soon I was an "expert" and I was doing all sorts of tricks. I must have been doing this for about 20 minutes when my older sister drove up in the old steel blue Ford station wagon. That was our family means of transportation at that time. "Hey kiddo! Want to go to the store with me?" she said. I smiled back at her, but for some reason, I felt uneasy. Something wasn't right, but I couldn't put my finger on it. I stood there and thought about it for a moment. I was leaning towards going with her, as we always had a great time together, but for some reason I felt nervous and uneasy. She asked me, "What's wrong?' I gave her my answer. "Well, for some reason I really don't want to go. I think I'll just stay here and play with my glider." This was kind of strange, I thought at the time. (I was somehow being given a message internally to continue flying my glider). She looked back at me and gave me the same look I was giving her. I've always been one to trust my instincts and this time was no different. We then smiled at each other and she said, "Ok then. See you in a little bit".

I watched her drive away and go 3 blocks to the edge of William Land Park. It was a straight line from where I was standing, so it was easy to follow the car. I thought to myself, "I wonder why I didn't go with her this time?" Oh well... I went back to flying my glider. Suddenly, and without warning, I heard this terrific CRASH sound. It was coming from near where I had last seen sis. I couldn't really see what was going on there, as it was too far away, but people seemed to be moving about very quickly. I ran home and let my Mom know. "I think sis just got hit in a car accident." "What?" She threw on her jacket and raced out the door to help her out. I pointed out to Mom where it happened. She looked for a moment, as sirens blared and ant-sized people rushed here and there, and then, silence. Mom hastily rushed down the street and to the aid of my sis.

Thank goodness, turns out sis was only hospitalized

with multiple cuts and bruises and she survived ok, but the exact place I would have been sitting was now no more than a crumpled massive hunk of metal, with a nicely shaped "C" curve. On the right front passenger seat, right where her car was hit by the other car, I would have been sitting. Thank goodness I followed my instincts and listened to my "gut feelings". Whew! That was a close one...My sister, well she went to the hospital and was there for awhile, but she healed up fine.

I have one thing to add. People have asked me, from time to time, "When do you know if you should follow your instincts?" This is my answer. If you get a repeated direct positive urging, **follow** that. If you get a warning of dire circumstances **never** listen to that. For example, those people who felt the uncontrollable urge to "get a cup of coffee" and be a bit late for work, had their lives saved by following that guidance, when the twin towers crashed... Or, the little old lady driving the car, that felt the uncontrollable repeated urging to "pull to the side of the road - NOW" and did so, lived, as others crashed into the stalled semi truck on the freeway. Or how about the guy that was about to go on a job interview and all of a sudden he got "the runs" and couldn't leave his home?

Well, because he was there he saved his daughter from choking to death. The list goes on…

On the other hand, if you either hear or feel something like "Watch out for that!" or "You're so afraid. You'll never be able to do that." Don't ever follow that, as it's coming from another place and promotes fear and uncertainty, which is the last thing needed right then.

It gets pretty comical sometimes when I go to find a parking spot and I am given the guidance to "Drive down this row" or "Drive around the block again" and do so. There, right up front, someone pulls out, and I get the perfect parking spot. Ain't life grand?

Sometimes things happen in other ways. You may be in a bookstore. You walk down a row and all of a sudden a book falls off the shelf at your feet. "Hmmmm, that is just what I wanted to read!" Smile…

Red Daisies in The Snow

It was the summer of '73 and the decision had been made by my parents that a nice trip across Canada would be our next great family adventure. I was totally up for this and couldn't wait to get on the road. We all packed up our things in duffel bags my Mom had sewn and stored them in the family Ford camper. Pop and Mom sat downstairs in the cab, while my twin and I were inside the camper, riding up top, laying on sleeping bags, overlooking the cab. The scenery was simply breath-taking. You get a view of things up high like that that is so different from what one normally sees. Now I kind of understand why truck drivers like their job so much.

A few days went by and I was noticing that there were fewer and fewer vehicles on the road and the air seemed to get more and more fresh and crisp. We drove around one winding curve and all of a sudden tall mountains appeared before me. These were the famous Canadian Rockies I had heard so much about. I started to notice snow along the side of the road and then, after a final turn, there it was, the majestic Lake Louise. I looked on in awe. I couldn't wait to get out of that camper! I climbed down the steps and jumped onto the ground. What a view before me!

"Now what should I do?" I thought. "I can either go get something to eat over at the lodge or I can swim in the Lake. No, that won't do. I want to go for a hike. It's simply gorgeous out here." I looked all over to find a trail and finally found it. I walked on over and started my journey. Tree bark marked the route on the sides and even under my feet. The smell was like freshly cut wood. Love that! At first the trail was rather flat but as I hiked further it gradually started angling upwards. I went further and further away from all civilization. At one point I got to the tree line. The view cleared, and I looked down at the lake. I could see people, as small as ants, paddling canoes in the aqua colored water. The kids were laughing and all seemed to be having a great time. I turned around and got back to business and started hiking again. The trail went from kind of a brownish muddy color to the start of patchy snowy ground. From there, it started to get rockier, with even more snow. Also, the trail started to wind and corkscrew around the mountain up, up, way up high. I struggled and slowly I trudged ahead. Before me I was now seeing tall spires of boulders. The trail was now quite a challenge and I was walking even more slower and slower. Thick snow now heavily blanketed the path before me. This was going to be a chore…Snow started to actually go up my legs a bit as I gradually moved forward. I looked down at one point and I saw what looked like small red flowers, like daisies, in the snow. First, there were maybe one or two, but then I noticed there seemed to be more and more. I wondered, "What's this?" Seems like I walked for miles around the mountain and all the while I was seeing more of these red daisies. And then, it happened. As I was about to make my way around this one large tree that was completely covered in snow I looked up, and what did I see? There, right in front of me, stood a VERY large brown bear. He appeared to be about maybe 7 feet tall and he was standing on his hind legs, with his front paws outstretched to the side, like a giant cross. My, what long fingernails he had! He looked at me in amazement and I returned the same look. We were both surprised to see each other in this place. I took a quick scan of his entire body and as I looked down at his right paw when he was standing, I noticed something. Right where his knee would be, hard to tell, as it was so hairy, it looked like he had gotten injured in some way. I don't know if he was shot. I don't know if he scraped up against something or fought with another animal or what happened, but he was bleeding and quite a bit. What I had thought were "red daisies" in the snow was actually his blood! Yes, I know what you're going to say. "What did you do?" What you're never supposed to do! You're never supposed to run away from a bear, as they can easily outrun you, but in this case, it WAS the right thing to do. I turned around and ran as fast as this body could go. I was freaked! I don't think I've been so afraid in all my life. It must have taken me only about half an hour to get all the way back down the mountain. It had taken me about two hours to get where I previously had been. I was shaking with fear and relief that I had made it down alive. I know. You're wondering, "Did he chase after you? What happened to the bear?" Nope, he couldn't chase after me. He was simply too injured to follow and I don't know what happened to the bear. I just hunkered down inside the camper, with a cozy comfy blanket around me and mom's nice warm chicken noodle soup to warm me up. Everyone I've talked with since has said the same thing. "You're NEVER supposed to run from a bear!" Well, let's see what YOU would do if faced with this...All I can say is that it was the right thing to do in that particular moment. To do anything else, well... I wouldn't even be writing this.

I've looked back on this adventure from time to time and just smile... Can you imagine? What a close one that was! I wonder what's next?

Bay of Fundy Adventure

The year was 1976. My parents decided to take a trip up through Canada and travel the scenic highway. My younger brother and I were asked if we would like to come along. Are you kidding? You bet! I love to travel and see new things and meet new people.

One week later the 4 of us were on our way. Of all the memories from that trip, of which there were many, one stands out from the others. You will soon see why.

You see, at one point we arrived at a place I had heard and read much about. I didn't know the significance of it at the time, but as I found out later, my Acadian ancestors lived here in this place in the mid 1600's. It's a magical place. The air is fresh and clean and the Atlantic Ocean is very different from the west coast Pacific Ocean. The water is rough, churning and unforgiving. Yes, this was the famous Bay of Fundy on the East Coast I had heard so much about. It has the highest tides in all the world. Boy, was I ever about to learn that!

My parents had arranged the trip in such a way that we would spend one day in each area to be discovered, but this area was different. I wouldn't let them leave for 3 days time. I somehow felt drawn to the place and couldn't get enough of it.

We set up the tent and campsite and relaxed in the lawn chairs. Soon, I was getting hungry. My younger brother and I decided to see if we could catch some fish for dinner. We gathered up our rods and tackle and off we went. There was a small trail near our campsite so we decided to take that, as it seemed to lead in the direction of the water. You could hear the ocean through the woods, so we followed the sound and at one point the area cleared and then, directly in front of us was the Salmon River, which is a tributary of the Bay of Fundy. We set up our poles and put on the bait and waited for the fish to bite. It wasn't long before something else bit…

I was standing there, rod in hand, with the Bay to my right, off in the distance, and my brother to my left. All of a sudden I heard this sound to my right, much like a loud yawn, and looked in complete AWE as this wall of water, maybe 12 feet high, was raging towards the two of us, at lightning speed. The wall of water was about 50 yards away but there wasn't much I could do. I dropped everything and started up the steep embankment. Hesitating for a moment, I looked back, reached over and down, and yanked a fist full of collar of my brother's coat. "What are you doing?" he yelped. "Saving your life." He suddenly was being overtaken with water and quickly it rose, right up to his waist. It took all I could muster to haul him backwards, up and out of danger. I pulled, back, back, back and then when I knew we were out of the way of the wave we both fell backwards and on to the ground in safety. The water raged past us and continued on. We stood up there and watched, as everything in the watery path was swept away! This was maybe 4 feet away from where we were now standing. We looked at each other and just shook our heads slowly from side to side. That was enough excitement for one day. We grabbed what we had left and made it back through the woods and back to the campground. A park ranger saw us as we came out of the woods into the campground complex. He stopped to talk. "Why are you two all wet?" "We were fishing and the water came in and almost drowned both of us." "What? Didn't you see the signs? NO FISHING. DANGEROUS CURRENT. "We didn't see any signs. We just took the trail, right next to our campsite".

It so happened that every day at this time, the ocean releases her energy and water races from the Bay of Fundy into the Salmon River and beyond. When there is a Full Moon the tides are even more severe. Thank goodness I was aware of my surroundings and I did something right away when I saw that wall of water. Otherwise, I wouldn't even be writing this right now….

So, pay attention to your surroundings and be in the present. It's a gift you give to yourself.

Fishing anyone?

High Noon at 12 Midnight

Several years ago I lived in Sacramento, California. There was much to see and experience there. One day, I decided to explore a place called Old Sacramento, all by myself. This was an area of town that used to be the center of all activity when the city was first founded, back in 1849. You could see a glimpse of what it might have been like back then. The outer "skeleton" of each establishment appeared to have the same shape it would have had back then. As I walked along the middle of the dusty cobblestoned street I could just picture what it must have been like in "49er" days, and imagined all the gold that must have come through this part of town. This was the famous gold rush we have all heard so much about in school. The buildings around me appeared not to have changed that much since then and I felt like I was back in the old wild west. I decided to explore most of the establishments and spoke with all sorts of people on a variety of subjects. Time flew by and before I knew it the clock struck 12 midnight. It was time to leave and head home. I decided to check out one more place before I left. "That looks interesting. Wonder what's inside?" I thought. There was this place up ahead and the design of it made me very curious as to what was inside. As I was walking I looked over to my left. I decided it would be fun to walk instead over the old wide wooden slatted walkway, that was directly next to each of the buildings. There were spaces between the slats and I could only imagine what treasure might be hidden underneath them. This would have been the walkway used when someone was coming to weigh the gold that had been found.

As I stepped up on to the old wooden platform a "block of thought" came rushing into my head. "**Turn around and look straight into his eyes**." I thought this was an odd thing to hear, but if you have been through what I've been through over the years you wouldn't doubt the help being given. I immediately followed the advice and spun around. A man, unshaven and about 6 feet 2, was rushing quickly towards me, with what appeared to be a large knife in his hand. Imagine his surprise when all of a sudden I looked not only at him, but also DIRECTLY in to his eyes. His demeanor changed from one of overbearing and quick aggression to a look of sheer terror and he immediately slid with both feet to a complete stop. As I continued to glare at him he quickly got hold of himself and hurriedly collected himself, turned around in the opposite direction and scampered quickly out of my sight. Periodically, I reflect back on this moment in time, and wonder what might have been going through his mind when I suddenly spun around and looked directly at him. Was it just the fact of me looking directly at him that made him change his mind? Or did he see something around me or above me, protecting me? It was like I became like a mirror for him and all the fear he was trying to impart upon me was reflected back directly at him. All I know is that the look on his face was priceless. I've never seen anything like it before or since. Sheer terror. He had done a complete 180 degree turnabout.

Wow, if I hadn't listened to that voice in my head and followed the directions EXACTLY I would either have been bloodied and in great pain or quite likely dead. It still amazes me, even today, that this even happened. It is a reminder to me and all of us that we are always being watched over, even when we consider we may not be. We alone decide on how close that connection will be. For some, they might just get a feeling. For others, when they're ready, it just might be a still small voice, or more. Many times we have that close connection when we are very young and then society pushes us to "grow out" of it. If they only knew…

I know what you are about to say. "So why is it that so many go through so much suffering and pain?" I can only say that for me I at one point very passionately and with great intention decided that I wanted to be guided by the highest of the high, the holiest of the holy, the wisest of the wise. That I will always be directed, in the most appropriate way for me, for the betterment of my life and those with whom I come in contact. It might be that I simply give someone a smile or even just say "Hello!" but it all makes the journey all the easier. You never know when that smile or "hello" you give totally changes the direction of a person's life….

So, I know you're going to ask this also. "How do I know if I hear a voice if I should follow what it says?" This is crucial. Any communication you get from the other side that makes you feel afraid, in fear, nervous or distrusting, well, that comes from a place I am not interested in. We'll let the "experts" discuss all about that. You want to put your attention on what you want instead of what you don't want. It's the Law of Attraction at work here. That communication you get that makes you feel confident, loving, at peace, playful and decisive and strong, now that I follow. For example: "Buy that fruit. You're hungry." I would follow that advice probably. But if I hear or feel "Watch out for that car!" Nope. You see the difference. One gives clear concise direct and repeating positive directions. The other gives a general, imprecise, and disturbing wording or feeling. Remember, you must pre-pray how you want your help. Otherwise, you will just get just about anything. What I mean by this is let's say you feel comfortable receiving messages in the form of "blocks of thought." Go that route. Or maybe you feel more comfortable receiving an actual voice. Ask for that to help out. Maybe a gentle whisper in your ear or that "gut feeling" we sometimes get. It will be different for each person what feels best. The important thing is to ask to connect in the most comfortable way for you and then trust and believe that it will happen. I can't tell you how many times I've spoken with someone who was just about to have an encounter like this and then they became afraid when things started to happen. They then either spoke out loud or inside their head for that which spoke with them to leave because they had been taught anything like this was coming from a negative place. What if it wasn't? What if it was coming from the all knowing, all seeing, all feeling creator? Yes, you know what I mean. You do deserve this. You are appreciated more than you know. Remember, you asked for this. Trust in the process. Focus and be persistent. Meditation in one form or another for 15 minutes a day, at whatever time is convenient for you, will speed up the process. Your passion, persistence and desire to connect also has great value in the process. Imagine a day when you wake up and thank the Creator for everything in your life and you get an answer back DIRECTLY. Yes, that is possible.

The other thing I want to share here is that when a miracle occurs many times we get all excited and this pushes away that which we seek. Remain centered and balanced if possible. Like everything, this takes practice.

Ever get the feeling like you should change lanes, while in traffic? There's a reason for it. So pay attention.

8

Well Blow Me Down

I remember this like it happened yesterday....

This story will relate to many hikers, especially anyone who has ever hiked Mount Hood in Oregon. It was late May. The day began innocently enough, as my buddy and I ate a quick hearty breakfast. Sometimes oatmeal REALLY hits the spot in the cool, crisp early morning! It did on this particular day. It was the weekend and we had both wanted to get out in nature and hike around to see what we could see. Several places came to mind. There was Mount Adams, Mount Jefferson and Mount St Helens, to name a few. We both decided Mount Hood would be our next adventure. We loaded up our food, supplies and extra clothes in our respective backpacks and threw them in the car. We jumped in, buckled up and off we went. It was a brilliant beautiful summer day. Not a cloud was in the sky. It was as blue as could be. The sun felt good and warm and I was looking forward to exploring the mountain. My buddy drove and it took about an hour to get to the lodge. We both dressed into hiking shorts and a T-shirt, then put on heavy duty hiking boots and slung on our backpacks. We didn't know exactly what to expect but we had this "inner instinct" to pack extra clothes in our backpacks, so we did just that. Remember this. It's important.

Amazingly enough we didn't run into any other hikers, a rarity on that mountain. I wonder why that was? Oh well… We took the Southern trail, as that side of the mountain had a flat trail, but gradually climbed up, up, up. The trail on both sides had a very steep scree slope. I took a moment and tossed a small pebble onto it, to see what might happen. I found out very quickly, as I watched the small pebble now become 8, 12, 20 or more, now gathering momentum and taking up everything in it's path as it rolled down the hill. If you were unfortunate and took one misstep, down you would go, skiing on all the small rocks, and into a snowy crevasse. So, we were very careful with each step and proceeded further up the mountain. The trail we took angled upwards, and we plodded slowly along, taking in all the sights and smells. After a couple of hours we were getting tired and decided to take a break and drink some water. So we stopped for a moment. The air was clean, the sky was blue, but boy, was it hot! We stood there for a moment and got our fill of cool icy refreshment - ice water. Then, we both had a great idea and poured some over our heads to cool off. We stood there a moment and basked in the sun. Ah, what a feeling that was…

All of a sudden we heard this very strange noise, like a very large yawn, coming from the far West end of the Willamette Valley on our left. We looked over to see what was going on. Our eyes BULGED out with surprise! We could see in the far distance bolts of lightning shooting down from darkened clouds and now we were also hearing thunder. The sky over there was smoky black and was swirling with intense movement. We took one quick look at each other and both said in unison, "Let's get out a here!" We quickly opened up our backpacks and as we ran back down the mountain, out came our long pants, long sleeve shirts, and heavy jackets. We stopped for a short moment to get them on, hopping as quickly as we could to get our pants on, and then continued running down the hill. In what seemed like a matter of minutes the storm was directly over us and we were now being just PELTED with rain, sleet and wind. Our clothes were completely drenched by this time and we were both shivering uncontrollably. It took maybe only half an hour for us to get back down the slope safely, but quickly, so you can see just how fast the storm was upon us. We jumped in the car and threw off everything and changed into dry clothes. Luckily for us, we prepared for anything, so we even had a couple of large white plastic bags to put our wet clothes in. Yes, we were shivering, but we were now dry and each of us had a large blanket around us. We felt relieved the drama was over, as we looked at each other and laughed. Whew, that was a close one! Imagine if we hadn't followed our instincts to pack extra clothes and a blanket and food. Do you know how many people have died on that mountain when a storm like this suddenly comes in? Guess it would have helped if we both checked the weather report for that area. That was the last time I hiked Mt Hood in May…

So, prepare your hike, but plan for the unexpected. A lot like life…

The Last Gasp

You know, at one point in time I worked as a carpet cleaner for a major company. Well, I was just turning in my work papers and money from my route that day at the front desk, when my boss came bursting into the main room with a big smile on his face. "Say, would anyone like to go on a group excursion to the Deschutes River and go on a raft trip?" I Immediately raised my hand up high in the air and gave a big smile. "What do you have in mind?" I asked. He replied, "Well, I was just talking with my cousin. (He was currently our mechanic, who worked on all our company vans.) You know he used to be a guide on that river many years ago. I've never been on a raft trip before and I would like to get a group of us from work and go share a day of excitement on the river."

"You bet! I'm in!" And then I thought, "What am I thinking?" I'd never been on a raft trip before myself. Hah, was I in for a surprise…

I got on the internet and looked at a map of the area. There it was, the Deschutes River. The town nearby was named for a French-Canadian trapper, Howard Maupin, who had a farm and a ferry in the early 19th century. Boy, did the river ever have some twists and turns. I made up my mind right then that I would be in the raft of the most experienced guide, our company mechanic, so there wouldn't be any problems. Finally, the day of the raft adventure came and friends and family alike decided to come along and help out. There was to be a fun company picnic when all the rafting was over and families brought all sorts of yummy food. Those of us who were going down the river in the two rafts were dropped off by family members and friends at the top part of the river. I jumped in one car with my buddies and it just so happened all 6 of us passengers decided to be in one raft. The wife of my guide was driving the car and she dropped us all off with the raft and supplies at the top part of the canyon. Then she drove down the dusty road to the bottom parking lot to join with the driver of the other car, who had also just dropped off the occupants of the second car. Other friends and family met them at the bottom parking lot. Then, they waited for those of us in the rafts to come down the river and some even decided to sun themselves in various places along the river and watch all that was about to happen or even take photographs with their cameras.

I recall that I was given specific instructions by the guide. We all huddled together on the bank and he went over everything before we climbed into the large rubberized raft. "Everyone has to wear a life jacket, no exceptions." He meant business but that's exactly what I wanted to hear. "I will be in the very back of the raft, guiding it with an oar as we go. Talk among yourselves and decide where you would like to sit. Now, as we come down the river, there will be places where I will give specific directions. Follow exactly what I say and we'll be fine. I want everyone to use the oars in unison. The beginning will be fairly flat, with a few whitecaps here and there. As we go down the river the current will get rougher and rougher. I will guide us to various places on either side of the river, so we safely make our way. There will be a place, about half way down the river, where we will stop and get out, and take a look from the bank at what we've just accomplished. Are there any questions? No? Ok, Let's all get started." We all donned our orange safety jackets that were made available and the anticipation and excitement was high as to what might come next. "Oh, I almost forgot," exclaimed the guide. "There will be one spot in the river where, if you decide to, you can literally jump in the river. You put your body in a sitting position, with the tennis shoes you are wearing facing downstream. That way, if you hit a boulder or object of some sort you can easily push off again." That made sense. We all looked at each other and there were two of us who were up for the challenge. One of them was yours truly. The raft was then filled with air with a mechanical electric pump and we all lifted it up in unison and carried it to the waters edge. To get a clear picture of what the raft looked like, all the outer extremities were blown up with air to the point where you were surrounded by 2 gray torpedo-like appendages. Around all the edges were large attached circular grommets. Through all of them was this thick white sturdy rope which was also securely fastened. We were instructed to hold on to the rope if we ran into trouble at any point in the journey. The bottom of the raft was flat and very thick. The guide slowly pushed our "ship" in the water and tied it off with a rope to a tree. "Ok, it's time to all get in." We all carefully and methodically got in to the large gray pontoon raft. I sat on the right side, near the rear, in front of the guide. When everyone had entered and sat down we were given instructions about the oars. "When you get the oar pay close attention to what and who is around you. Either have the oar flat on the bottom of the raft or use it in the water. I don't want anyone getting hurt. Now, when I tell you, pick up your oar slowly and stand it straight up next to you. This is the position you are in before we start to raft." He gave a signal nod and we all grabbed hold of our respective oars and placed the base on the floor of the raft and stood them all straight up. The guide then asked, "Is everyone ready?" We all smiled and in unison gave a big fist pump in the air. "Yes!" The guide picked up his own oar and gently pushed off from shore. We all let our oars tip slowly down and into the water and we were on our way!

The beginning part of the trip was pretty tame and there was a lightly sloping plane downwards. Small whitecaps dotted our way downstream. The air was fresh and not a cloud was in the sky. "Can't get better than this," I thought. Now as far as the river was concerned, it wasn't that cold, but it sure was moving fast. The scenery was perfect. People were laying out on boulders, sunning themselves. Some were eating snacks, some were having a soft drink, and still others, a beer. Everywhere you looked there was something to see. The river was wide in some parts and then corkscrewed and churned into thinner chutes. The land around us varied also. At times there were spires of boulders and then in a few minutes the land had sloped downwards and you had low growing grassy areas. We lollygagged and splashed water on each other from time to time as we went. We even got to this one place where you could see the remnants of volcanic activity. The ground on shore was completely solid black so we took a few moments to stop and investigate the area. What an odd place this was. Everywhere you looked here the ground was shiny but uneven. Plants were trying to grow where they could, through but they were few and far between. We climbed back in the raft and off we went again.

The further on we traveled the waves became bigger. Pretty soon there were several small "waterfalls" we had to traverse and go over. We made it through just fine however. The guide did a GREAT job of preparing us for everything. I almost forgot. He warned us that there is this one place in the river called "Elevator". Bet you can't guess why it is called that! So we were prepared for pretty much everything, except for what happened to the two of us that jumped into the river... We passed some more volcanic boulders on shore and all sorts of wonderful colored rocks and scenery. Others in rafts near us were laughing and also enjoying the day. Some passed us up. Others were guided to go down the river much slower than us. So onward we went. Pretty soon, the river got wide again and on the right side of the river tall jagged boulders faced us. The guide mentioned, "We are about to get to Elevator. What do you think?" Silence. He quickly eyed everyone and decided it was best to go the safe route. So he angled left across the tall whitecaps and we dove straight downwards for a moment or two, and then up we popped and finally tapered off to a point were we were in a lateral position again. Whew, that was scary...

We all buzzed with excitement and looked back at what we'd just gone through. Did we really do that? Yes, we did!

Suddenly, I noticed there were more and more black

boulders sticking out of the water, and we were getting dangerously close to running into a few of them. The guide tried his darndest to keep us righted and going in the correct direction. At one point we did float up against one of these massive imposing jagged boulders. We were pinned up against it for a short moment. The guide nicely and expertly stuck out his oar and us pushed off and we were back on our way again.

We then floated further down steam. Our guide mentioned that we were now at the point where one could jump into the water. It was time to "make our leap". My buddy decided to go first. He bent over and laid his oar flat in the bottom of the raft. Then, he stood straight up in the middle of the raft, smiled at all of us, and said, "Here goes!" He planted one foot near the edge of the left side of the raft and jumped in quickly but methodically, so as not to tip over the raft. Splash! He rose to the surface and his body bobbed up and down. He faced the raft briefly and watched me, as I jumped in next. I stood up, laid down my oar in the bottom of the craft also. Then, I put my right foot near the edge of the right side of the raft and jumped in. Splash again! My body disappeared under the water but then bobbed back up, just like my buddy. I was floating about 15-20 feet behind him. The raft meanwhile, sped up due to the current and less weight. The guide urged it onward to the left side of the river and hastily my other friends raced down the river. We both waved happily at everyone in the raft as they disappeared out of sight.

We were both now in the middle part of the river. My buddy was turned around and faced me upstream. Suddenly, "SCHLUP!". My buddy disappeared below the surface. It was like someone took his legs and just yanked him under the water. No warning. Nothing. It happened so fast he didn't even have a chance to take a deep breath before he went under. I recall it happened so fast, in fact, that he only had time to raise his left arm up high to let me know he was in distress and in trouble. He stayed under. "Great!" I thought. "I hope he'll be ok." I now had my own predicament to think about. For you see, the current was now bringing me to that same spot! I did have a moment to collect my thoughts so I decided I better take a VERY deep breath when I reached that point. I bobbed, weaved and floated to the same spot shortly and in a manner of seconds (Deep breath) I too was pulled under the water, straight down. And yes, it WAS like someone was pulling my legs down to the bottom of the river. (Wonder if it was my buddy...?) The view under the water was not what you would call "scenic". All I could see was swirling murky, muddy water and that's it. I panicked and frantically I swung my arms here and there, trying in vain to reach the surface again and again, but it seemed the more I struggled the more worn out I became. I HAD to make it. I simply had to make it. I wasn't ready to die! I placed my hands together in front of me, with palms outward, like a reverse prayer, and pushed the water from the center to the sides. I tried everything, even dog paddling, but nothing seemed to work. I fought with the water for what seemed like forever, until I reached the point where I simply was all tuckered out. I gave it one last ditch effort but I simply couldn't hold on any longer. I was done. Or was I? All of a sudden I got this message in a block of thought and then I heard distinctly the two words, "LET GO!" I don't know where this came from, only that it did happen and I'm glad it did. There had been several other times where I had gotten messages in this manner and I had listened and followed the advice and all turned out ok, so I had nothing to lose. I said the quickest prayer you ever prayed, "Ok God, if I am to die now, so be it, but if I am to live, it's all in your hands." I made myself stop fighting the current and everything else and simply closed my eyes, relaxed, and let go, fully and completely, and my body went from being like wiggly Jello to becoming completely limp. Instantly, my body turned totally upside down and shot straight up, just like a bullet, towards the surface. Yes, you guessed it. I had gotten so confused under the water that I thought down was up and vice versa. I reached the surface VERY quickly and broke through the water, like a shark, to the clean fresh air, took a quick gasping breath and crashed back down to the surface. Up and down I bobbed. I gasped and gasped for air...Ahhhhhh ... THAT'S more like it! I gobbled up more air and the current brought me safely to the left side bank. I lay there on the watery rocks for a moment, on my stomach, limp as could be, and thanked God for saving my life. THAT was a close one!

But then, I came to my senses and realized, "Where's my buddy?" I got up and looked back at the river. He was no where to be found. I waited. It seemed like 15 seconds turned into what felt like hours, only it wasn't. Suddenly, he also broke through the surface, but on the opposite side of the river, and his body drifted to that shore. I saw him stay there a few moments, face down, to catch his own breath, until he too was concerned about me. He turned toward the river again. Instantly, we both pointed right at each other and laughed, for we both knew we shouldn't even be alive. I systematically hiked down the rocky left side of the canyon while he hiked down the right. We both made it to the bottom of the canyon and rejoined our group. The first thing they all said was, "What happened to you guys?" "Well, we almost died!" "What? You're kidding!" "Nope, we both nearly drowned!" Wouldn't you know it. No one believed us, but we know the truth.

Moral of the story? Sometimes "letting go" will get you through the tough times. You just have to stop yourself from "fighting" against the current, with what are your present circumstances. This may be quite controversial but my firm belief is that everything happens for a reason, in its own way, in its own time. We may not understand at the moment why things happen the way they do, but the Creator has a plan, and later on, with reflection, you suddenly realize why things happened the way they did. Many times things even repeat themselves in certain ways, until we finally learn the "lesson". Anyone want to go rafting?

Hit and Run

Ever go on a blind date? Well, this was a date like no other. One of a kind it was. You see, a mutual friend introduced us. My friend met this gal and decided it would be nice to have breakfast together. So she invited her new girlfriend to meet her at this nice cozy corner breakfast establishment. What I didn't know is my friend had a plan. I was called on the phone and asked if I were interested in meeting someone new. I thought about it a moment and decided to take the plunge and go. I hopped in the car and off I went. Shortly, I arrived and parked my car. I walked in the restaurant and found the two of them in the corner, sipping their hot coffees. I walked up, smiled, and said, "Do you have room for one more?" "Of course," came the reply. So I pulled out a chair and sat down and began my visit. Somehow the food tasted especially good that day… The meal ended with pleasant conversation and before I left I was given her name and phone number and was asked to call some time the next week. Fast forward. I called her up and picked her up at her place and we went out to eat at a nice Italian Restaurant. I had the Tour of Italy. Everything was perfect: the food, the company, the service. We finished dinner and it was now time to leave. We picked up our things, I paid the bill and out to the car we went. We drove off and started to discuss the great meal. Boy that was good!

We were traveling in my cream colored Toyota Corolla about 35 miles an hour, the speed limit there, when all of a sudden we were rammed into from behind so hard that it picked up the car and threw it maybe 10 feet forward. I still recall the slow motion of the car arching up through the air, my back pressed firmly against the back of the seat, and the feel of the parabola curve, as the car came down to the ground with a clump clump. I knew right then I was hurt, and hurt bad. My date was injured also, but I wasn't sure exactly how much. I slammed on the brakes and came to a complete stop. I looked in the mirror to the driver behind. Wouldn't you know it? The guy that plowed into me had stopped, then he backed up, made a letter "C" around my car to the left of us, and floored it. I looked at my date and exclaimed, "Hold on and call the cops! We're going to catch him. I'm going to make sure he never does this to anybody else again." She couldn't believe it. Yes, I know. Pretty stupid huh?

I floored it and took off in hot pursuit, placing my right hand on the horn, so everyone would get out of the way. People in cars and bystanders on the sidewalk looked on in consternation. Meanwhile, try as he could, the man I was chasing in the car in front of me couldn't shake me off his tail. He darted here and there, trying to lose me. Nothing doing... I stayed a safe distance behind him but stuck to him like glue. We drove for about a mile and ended up driving in the shape of a large square and back on the same road we started. He finally realized he wasn't going to lose me so he slowed down, pulled in to an apartment complex and parked in the closest space. Turns out my date was the Manager of that specific apartment complex. Can you imagine? What are the odds… I pulled in right behind him and stopped my car directly sideways to the back of his car, so it blocked him in. I opened my car door and jumped out of my car, furious. I'm not a tall sort, maybe 5'5". The guy in the car in front of me exited his car and walked towards me, head down. He was probably 6'3 and about 260 pounds but he cowered like a puppy dog when I walked right up to him. I pointed my finger at him. "What were you thinking?" I asked. "I'm sorry. It's all my fault," he replied. "We'll talk about that later. Go get your proof of insurance from the car and bring that and your drivers license back, so we can exchange information." I turned back around and went back to get mine. I opened my driver's door and poked my head in and bent over and quickly gathered my info from the glove box and looked up. You'll never guess what I saw? Yep, You guessed it. All 4 doors of that car were now wide open and out had raced 4 big men from each door, who then took off running across the open field away from me. Each one was over 6 feet tall and all were heavy set. Obviously I wasn't thinking straight at the time, I was so angry. I chased after all of them on foot, and as they fanned out in different directions I kept my eyes glued on the driver. "Come back here!" They could have turned around and beaten the living daylights out of me had they wanted, but they didn't. The driver was the closest to me, about 20 yards away, and at one point he turned sideways to his right and looked back at me, while running. "Stop!" I yelled. "You better come back and take responsibility for what you did. You've really injured two people." He wryly smiled, smirked at me, then turned back around and poured on the speed and raced off and out of sight. I finally came to my senses, slowed down, and came to a complete stop. I realized there was no way I was going to catch him now, and besides, they could have done just about anything to me. I turned back around and slowly walked back to my car. Right when I arrived there two cops drove up, each in a separate car drove up, one on the left of me, one on the right and screeched to a halt. They hopped out and each pulled a gun. "Where are they?" Each had a German Shepherd on leash with the other hand. I pointed them in the direction of where I had last seen the offender and his cronies. They ran off in hot pursuit across the open courtyard but finding no one, returned in about 5 minutes. "What were you thinking?" they asked me. "I wasn't. I only know I am hurt really bad and she probably is too. I had to get the guy to take responsibility for what he did." The cops said you should NEVER chase after someone like this but, I was smart to block the guy in. They took down the information from his car he left and, as it turned out later, this WAS the owner of the car and he had done this before to someone else. I ended up suing the guy, as he kept hanging up on his insurance agent. In 3 days' time my body felt the full brunt of the turmoil I had just experienced. I experienced dyslexia, mental mood swings, couldn't do any math in my head at all and physically my left hip was thrown out, my feet hurt and I was in a great deal of pain in my lower back. I ended up not being able to work for over 7 months. It was real bad. Finally, after one year, the law suit was settled, I was now back to work, but I was still having problems with my memory. I made an appointment with my doctor and went to see him to get all checked out. He could see that physically I was ok now but somehow in the hit and run my brain had been "scrambled" as he put it. So then I was referred to a specialist to see what was up. Here I did some physical skill sets and more mental tests. Long story short, it was found I had not one but two brain concussions. It was explained to me my short term memory would probably never be the same again, but my long term memory would return. Still, I was having difficulty. The doctors didn't know what else to do. They had done everything they could. So, as anyone would have done, I started investigating all sorts of alternative avenues.

Shortly thereafter, I got out of bed one morning and I felt COMPELLED to go to a website called ancestry.com. I didn't know what I was doing there but I investigated everything about the site. I added in some family names, just like it says on TV and pretty soon I was well on my way to creating a fairly large family tree. Here's the funny thing. The more I've done genealogy over the years, the better my brain has worked. As you can imagine, the tree is fairly large now, as what once was a way to heal has now turned into a rather interesting exploration into how I came to be and how I relate to all others.

The lesson here is: I followed my intuition, once again. No telling in what shape I'd be in now if I had not started doing genealogy and then continued with it. Quite amazing once you think about it.

Yes, I know you are wondering about that guy that plowed into my car and what happened to him. Well, he was fined $1,024.00 for the hit and run and I don't know what happened to him after that, but he did lose the lawsuit and I was told he got some time in jail to reflect back on all he did. Yes, I won the won the lawsuit. It wasn't much, but that wasn't the point of it all. I don't think he will be doing anything like that again, any time soon, to anyone else… I may have saved someone's life.

No, I don't recommend chasing after people in your car or, for that matter, on foot. That was a pretty stupid thing to do, for sure. All sorts of things could have happened. I do try now to be very aware of everything around me and if I had done this then I might have avoided this incident altogether.

Pay Attention – We
Need to Talk

The year was 1992. It was a bright sunny summer day. My back was in a great deal of pain. The previous day, Friday, I was working in my usual job as a carpet cleaner.

I had been moving quite a bit of heavy furniture to clean behind things and now my body was paying for it. Over time, my back had gotten a bit of an "S" curve. Scoliosis is what they call it, and now was the time I decided to do something about it. I had found a great massage therapist in town a few previous weeks before and tried her out and things were definitely changing for the better. I had booked an appointment for Saturday at 1 pm. Finally, a chance to be without pain in my back!

I had relaxed that morning by laying out in my lounge chair, with the foot rest fully out and then later on watched the New York Knicks basketball game on TV. I looked up at the clock at one point and realized I'd better get ready for my appointment. I jumped up from the lounge chair and exclaimed to my wife, "I better get going or I'm going to be late. Can't have that!" I hurriedly got my wallet and keys to the car and started to head out the door but I remembered that there were 3 bills that I needed to pay. I had placed them on top of my bureau in the bedroom but they were already in envelopes, stamped and ready to go and just needed to be placed in the mail box. I went back and grabbed them up quickly and headed for the front door again. I passed by my wife again. "Be back in a bit!"

It usually took me 20 minutes to get to the 1 o'clock

appointments by 5 minutes to 1, so I would be a little bit early this time. I jumped in the car, put the 3 bills on the front passenger seat beside me, put my seat belt on, put the key in the ignition and turned the key. Varoom! Boy did that '66 Mustang sound good. I checked in the side mirrors and the rear view mirror. The coast was clear so I put the car in reverse and started backwards. Just then, something mystical and magical happened. "GO PAY THE BILLS. NOW!!" came this booming voice. "Huh?" I stopped the car and looked all around me. Nothing. What was that? No people on the street. No cars. Nothing. I thought to myself, "That was strange. I wonder what this is all about? Funny, just last week someone told me they had a similar experience and they followed the directions and everything turned out ok." I sat there a moment to figure it all out… It didn't make any sense and I couldn't figure it out… Oh well. I looked at the time. "Yikes, I'm going to be late!" I again put the car in reverse and started the car backwards again. "GO PAY THE BILLS. NOW!!" came the voice again. The voice sounded VERY similar to that. It was like I was in an empty room and I was being communicated with in a positive echoing fatherly manner. I definitely was being watched over but I had the distinct impression I needed to listen and follow his advice. Have you ever walked out in the country and sometimes you run across a stream that flows through a large round metal cylinder because there is an overpass that goes over the stream? You go inside the metal circle, with the water running at your feet. I have. I've let out a huge "Helloooo!" and wait for the echo. It's always there. Well, this voice was like that. Remember, I had those 3 bills on the passenger seat next to me? "Ok, ok, I thought, as I looked at my watch. I still have time to make it to the massage therapist on time." I reached over, grabbed the 3 envelopes, opened the car door and raced over to our house mailbox, placed them inside, shut the mailbox door, raised the flag for the mail carrier and rushed back to the car. I jumped in, put my seat belt on again and thought, "Hmmm, that was odd. What is going on? No matter. I'll figure it out later. I better get on my way. I still have time to make it, if I hurry."

I backed out into the street and started to drive forward. "GO GET SOMETHING TO EAT. YOU'RE HUNGRY!" What the heck? There was that voice again. I **was** hungry after all… I hate to admit it. This was amazing. Something very powerful was going on but I didn't realize at the time how significant this all would be. Now imagine if this happened to you. I'm just as skeptical as the next guy. Just because I hear a repeating voice in my head and around me how do I know it's coming from the right place, if you know what I mean? I tried to make sense of it all. The message came in a male voice but it surely wasn't me. That's for sure. It was done in such a way that I wasn't afraid at all. I'm not crazy and I haven't been drinking and I'm certainly not making this up. Well, I thought I better test it. "Ok", I said to myself (interesting choice of words here), "I'm going to floor it. I'm going to get downtown as fast as I possibly can. If I'm not supposed to be there on time, this voice will REALLY come booming in." I put the pedal to the floor and the car took off in a flash. I must have been going 60 MPH (on the one way road right next to the Max line of Portland, Oregon, called Burnside Street) so I wouldn't be a danger to others. No one was on the road or sidewalk in either direction. What happened next is simply hard to explain in words, but I'll try. "GO GET SOMETHING TO EAT. YOU'RE HUNGRY!!!" The voice had repeated again, with exactly the same words. It was a male voice, not my own. No one was around. No cars. Nothing. This time I paid close attention. The voice was coming from, believe it or not, inside my OWN head, but also OUTSIDE it too! Remember the movie

The Ten Commandments? God speaks to Moses from the mysterious burning bush. It was almost EXACTLY like that. The voice echoed, like a voice would sound, when saying "HELLOOOO….", inside of a vacant building. But this was different. No, you ask, I wasn't drinking or smoking any funny stuff and I certainly was not making this up, that's for sure. This was really happening. And the voice was not my own, that was clear also. I don't take drugs. Check. I'm in my right mind. Check. But what really set things apart was the intention. Not only did the voice say what it did, but it was done in such a way and with such specific direction that you couldn't ignore it, like when a parent says to a child "you ARE going to do this, aren't you!". I didn't mess with it this time. I drove directly to a "Wendy's Hamburgers" and got a burger, fries and a soft drink and munched them down. Boy, did that hit the spot! I WAS hungry…

That now settled, I jumped into the car, put on my seat belt for the last time and off I went to my appointment. I hastily looked at my watch. 5 minutes to 1. "Now I AM going to be late." I wondered why this all happened? "Obviously I wasn't meant to be there, otherwise I would be," I thought. I took my time getting there now and, believe it or not, no more voice! 20 minutes later I made it downtown and parked on the 4th floor of the parking structure, directly across the street from my destination. I locked the car and walked over to the elevator, which was close by, pushed the button for the ground floor. The door opened and I stepped in. Down it went. You can imagine how you would feel if all this happened to you. You're trying to make sense of it all, but it doesn't make sense... unless it does. I emerged from the elevator on ground level and walked across the first crosswalk to the corner and stepped up. "That was so amazing," I thought. I stepped down into the street and walked halfway across the second crosswalk, all the while in a complete daze. Then it suddenly hit me. "Suppose I hadn't listened to that voice. Where exactly would I have been?" I was now smack dab in The Present and I turned and looked behind me. I smiled.... There, in front of me, was a jewelry store on the corner. Yellow police tape was wrapped from there to the next corner and half way down the block. I saw this oriental gentleman, sporting a nice goatee, about halfway up the street, walking on the sidewalk towards the front of the store. I hurriedly walked up to him. "Excuse me Sir," I asked. "Do you know what happened?" He smiled, "You're lucky you weren't here 20 minutes ago at 5 minutes to 1. There was this guy that had a gun.

He walked into that jewelry store there on the corner and tried to robbed it. The cashier grabbed a gun from behind the counter and chased him outside. Six people were shot by the robber and they just took all of them to the hospital and the robber to jail. All that's left now is the yellow tape!" My jaw dropped. I realized then that if I had ignored that voice I probably would be dead. Kind of makes you think, doesn't it?

I thanked the man for explaining everything and turned around and walked back across the street and upstairs to the office of my massage therapist. "You probably know why I'm late, don't you?" She replied back, with a look of consternation on her face, "I don't know what you're talking about." I gave her a look of surprise and exclaimed, "Look out the window to the street below and across the street and tell me what you see." The look on her face was priceless. "What happened?" I went over what I've just explained and she just shook her head. "I didn't hear a thing." We both struggled to figure it all out. I checked the local newspaper, the radio stations and the nightly news. Nothing! That's impossible. You'd think someone would have said something. The only sense I can make out of it all is that the guy must have had a silencer on his gun and the ambulances didn't sound their sirens, as that was a time when they needed all the customers they could get downtown, as the economy was real slow, and the city was doing all it could to help all the business establishments there survive. Yes, I've had people tell me I was just imagining all this. Not a chance. It's not surprising people wouldn't believe me but it's not my job to convince anyone of anything. My job simply is to let people know what happened. I am definitely being watched over and protected. There's no doubt about that. Thank you God, for watching over me and guiding me. I would say this is definitely one of those mysteries in life we hear about from time to time. Thank goodness I listened and followed his advice. I think it's all part of the process of evolution and as time goes by I will come to fully understand what great significance there was here, as there are others like me out there too...

Miracle at Crater Lake

The year was 1992. My wife and I, as well as my Mother in law and Aunt, decided we wanted to go on a camping trip. The in-laws both had driven out to Portland, Oregon from Nebraska in a camper. They had heard all about Crater Lake and how scenic it was but had never been there before. I also had never been there myself. So we decided THAT would our target.

We got up the very next morning and went to the store to get food for the camping trip. When that was all done we came back and packed. Night came, and we went to sleep, knowing that in the morning we would all be off on our adventure. The next morning, I awoke and found it was perfect weather for the trip. We all ate a quick breakfast and got in our respective vehicles. The in-laws drove in the Ford camper while my wife and I followed in our '66 Ford Mustang.

The drive was long and we found ourselves finally arriving at the entrance to the circular road around Crater Lake, Oregon. My, what a sight! There were no clouds and the full moon was there to the left of our vantage point and to the right, we caught a glimpse of the lake. We started in, and as we drove, you could actually see the reflection of the entire full moon upon the lake. It was simply magical, majestic and calming. Sights such as this can be rare and I made sure I got my fill of all the serenity.

We drove in to about half way around the lake when all of a sudden the in-laws camper broke down. What should we do? We huddled ourselves together to create a plan of action. We all agreed that it made the most sense that the women should and would all stay in the camper, as they could stay warm, as it had a heater. I would go drive in the Mustang to find help.

It was 12 midnight now, and the full moon guided me back to the entrance. I was thinking, as I drove, that the road was actually very narrow, and at one point I reflected back on the time when we entered the road, and that there was one place where there was only room for one vehicle to pass. Thank goodness there was no one on the road! I was just about to come to that place and I thought to myself, "What should I do if someone is coming from the other direction? I can't go forward. I would hit him. I can't go to the left, because I will crash into those jagged boulders. I can't go to the right. I would drown in the lake. I can't back up and I certainly can't just stop. There's really no solution." Right then, yes, you guessed it. Some guy driving a pickup truck appeared on the rise right in front of me and he was booking! Not much time. I still remember the look on his face. He was all glassy eyed and he was most certainly drunk. He came flying over the rise towards me and his truck flew in the air six or 7 feet. I said the quickest prayer you ever said. "Ok, God, now's your time to shine. I'm going to totally trust that I'm going to live. I'm going to drive straight ahead and trust that somehow I'll live." As I got closer and closer to the truck a miracle happened. Here's where you'll probably say I was drunk, that I was on drugs or I was dreaming or I simply imagined it all. Nope. None of the above… All of a sudden my entire body AND my car became like see-through cellophane. My body and car became like Casper the friendly ghost. I could actually see THROUGH my arms, steering wheel and down through the bottom of the car, to the ground. It was like I suddenly was in some other dimension. It all happened so quick, yet it all seemed to play out like molasses, in slow motion. I continued forward, and as we came up upon each other suddenly my car and I were passing RIGHT THROUGH his truck. I can't tell you how this happened, only that it did. As I write this I remember the look on his face when I drove right through the left/middle of his truck. Our heads were about two feet away from each other. I passed through his car right where his passenger seat would be. Impossible, but it happened. He looked like he was seeing a ghost. We both turned our heads and looked at each other momentarily when I was almost right next to him and as I went past his body. I proceeded forward and when I got to the other side of his truck suddenly my body and my car again turned back solid, as before. I slammed on the brakes and came to a complete stop. I jumped out and went back to talk to the fellow. He also had slammed on his brakes and was also stopped. I walked up to the driver side door. The man sat there motionless but very much alive. His eyes were fixed straight ahead. His window was rolled up so I motioned with my right hand in a cranking circular motion for him to roll it down. He looked at me with consummate terror and shook his head from side to side. I talked through the closed window to him, "It's ok. I'm just like you. Roll the window down. I want to talk." He looked at me again and very sheepishly slowly rolled down the window. I noticed that he was no longer drunk and he spoke with clear conviction and very deliberately slowly got out of his mouth, "**Did what just happened…. REALLY happen?**"

I laughed and replied, not knowing exactly why, "Yes, it did. I just drove right through your car. I don't know how, only that I did. We should both be dead. I noticed that you were drunk and now you aren't. I bet you have a wife and a couple of kids at home, don't you?"

He looked at me in utter amazement. "How do you know that? That's exactly what I have!" he replied.

"Well, I guess this is your wake-up call. I know this

didn't happen for me. If I were you, I would never ever take another drink as long as you live. Go home now and love your family and appreciate them, like you never have before."

"Don't worry. I'm never drinking again, ever! I still don't believe this happened!"

I smiled and shook his hand and he turned his truck around and headed home. I sure hope he got the message… For the life of me, I don't know why I said what I said.

And I bet you are wondering…Yes, I did find a mechanic. He fixed the camper and we were on our way again, off for further adventures…

A good lesson in the Power of Pre-Praying and trusting in God.

Making this Up

It has come to my attention that some may think that what I have written is simply "make believe" and that I have made all this up. I even get this from members of my own family. I'll let you be the judge but think about it for a moment. Why would I place myself in the position of being laughed at, ridiculed, pointed at, disbelieved and talked about behind my back unless it was important for me to share what I have experienced? No, I never saw a "white light" or anything like that. I have talked with people who have however. They tell about seeing this when they die and then they meet someone who tells them they are not done and it's time to come back and finish their work. This has never happened to me so I am not the one to ask about that. My shared experience is all about what one can do before one gets to that point.

Acknowledgments

Heather Perry and Joe Anderson of Balboa Books, you've done an excellent job. What patience. I wouldn't have finished the book without your perfect guidance.

My entire family. We each have our own view of the world but we have similar roots. I have learned so much from all of you.

My twin sister. There is nothing that compares with the love of a twin. You can't be any closer than this and not be one person. I love you sis.

To all my teachers. It's been a long road, with many obstacles but the lessons learned have really come in handy.

All my friends and relatives on this side and on the other. You know who you are. For some, we may meet for only a short time, for others, a bit longer. And those on the other side, I will be with you again when my work is done. In the meantime, thank you all for all you do and for all your help and guidance.

God, in all forms. I give thanks every day for my very existence.

Life is precious. Never take it for granted. What is your life in the moment today may be totally different by tomorrow morning. Yes, it can be challenging, even downright upsetting, but with persistence and time your view of life can change and blossom into something quite miraculous. Have you ever wondered why some people have extreme life challenges, overcome them and go on to make a nice life for themselves? They never give up! Persistence pays off. I will say this. Never give up. No matter the challenges there is always light at the end of the road. I remember a time when I had extreme vertigo. You know, when you get real dizzy and loose your balance. It was pretty bad. I tried all sorts of things to correct it. Nothing worked. Later on, I had injured myself and had to go to physical therapy. One of the questions asked was "Do you ever get dizzy?" I answered back "All the time!" The therapist looked at the paper and saw my answer. Would you like to get rid of that? "Heck yeah!" By the time I left my dizziness was gone, but she gave me a paper which gave the steps to take to fix this yourself at home. One can learn all about this online. It's called the Epley Maneuver.

I also want to mention in passing something else that will be useful. It is said that there is not a cure for Cancer. I am not a doctor but I have run across someone who did cure herself of terminal breast cancer. You see, she came from China. She had breast cancer real bad and had to have an operation to save her life. When she awoke from the surgery the doctor gave her the news that there was nothing more that he could do and he told her basically that she had two weeks to live and to go home and die. She would have none of that. She looked all over the place for cures. No one had the answer. She tried all sorts of things. Nothing worked… til she talked to her brother on the phone in Hawaii. You see, he had testicular cancer. He was told he didn't have long to live. He however found out about Soaring Crane Qigong. He practiced this every day and he actually was getting better. He told his sister all about it. She flew over to Hawaii from China to learn all about it from him. She started applying it to herself that very day. The next few days were hard but she was determined not to give up. She exercised doing this for 6 hours straight every day for 8 months. At the end of that period she decided to go in and get an xray and see how things were going. The doctors were totally perplexed. They came back to her with the results. "You sure you had cancer? If you did it's totally gone!" The next day she opened up a practice and taught all sorts of people about Soaring Crane Qigong. Her name? Professor Chen Hui Xian. Luckily, she came to Portland, Oregon and was my teacher for awhile. To learn more, go to "The Medical Benefits of Soaring Crane Qigong" online. There, it will explain more about the amazing Professor Chen. So you see, never give up. I've run across all sorts of people who have been cured of "Incurable" diseases. There are solutions out there. You just have to turn over every rock to find them.

Edwards Brothers Inc.
Ann Arbor MI. USA
January 24, 2018